FixTheNation.com

=Volume One=

I0428724

By

John A. Jensen

=First Edition=

Author's Note

WARNING to all who read what follows. IT is not meant as an endgame solution for all the ills of government, society, and the pain you and I feel every day.

It is meant as a *starting point*. It is a beginning of a social dialogue to hopefully get to that endgame sooner, as opposed to later.

There is no right or wrong opinion, so my ideas or thoughts are not perfect- or by any means the only path for us to take.

My challenge to all who continue reading is to do so with an open mind, to read and evaluate on merit- not ones' political affiliation, to embrace a topic or several and provide insight or solutions- not just say how stupid an idea is.

My belief in life is simple. *Either you are part of the problem, or part of the solution.* **PICK ONE.**

If you want to be part of the problem, STOP now. *Go away.* Do not pass GO, Do not collect $200(great board game line). That is not mean-spirited, but as a way to save your time and my frustration. No part of Brainstorming involves people saying what doesn't work, how something "sucks", or bashing one political person/party or the other. It is pointless and a complete waste of time and energy for all concerned.

If you want to be part of the solution, PLEASE keep reading. America needs what you have to say. YOU have an obligation to help America get its 'MoJo' back, to help in a small way. Your Opinion DOES matter. Your voice needs to be heard, and the Endgame will be YOURS. I truly believe that the solutions for our struggles lie inside the American ingenuity of this great country. By coming together- we can create, unite and solve.

My first goal is to craft future editions of this book based on feedback of the readers. YOU will help me try and bring a well-thought, well-rounded American blueprint to the life we want, the country we need.

My ultimate goal is to create a fulfilling social website, one that MATTERS. Not just a friend's medium, but a web connection that truly makes a difference- THAT is what has been missing in our country for years. We need a true national platform for us to come together, air the concerns and suggestions, vote and veto, mold and trim, add and delete- until we end up with the best possible suggestion.

Then- **WE MAKE OUR VOICES HEARD TO EVERY PUBLIC LEADER WE PUT INTO OFFICE**.

After all, we vote them in to represent us- right?

Remember- part of solving something is being willing to consider other options, be willing to compromise, and be willing to give and take. The bulk of Americans live in the big Moderate middle ground in most respects- not on either extreme. Funny that now politically, the ends are well-represented- but the middle of the political bell-curve is largely unrepresented. THAT is what needs to be addressed before all else.

So- if you are up for it, start reading and let me know what you think. The goal is not for me to have the right answer, but for us to get what works in the end. THAT part I will help with- but you will need to do.

Enjoy!

Federal Budget

Step One- write it.   *Step Two- pass it.*

That this was forgotten, or ignored, by our recent Political leaders *for over 2 ½ years* is tragic.

When you run a business or government you need to anticipate costs and revenue, keep them inline with each other, and make tough decisions fluidly to keep them in check. A budget is a piece of the puzzle in helping to do that very thing. It is a blueprint or guide of how you expect to spend and collect money. The people who elect you have a right to know how you intend to spend and collect, how you choose to overspend and run a deficit, and a right to know where your priorities are. A budget in part helps define your economic actions. When you don't have one, it hides this from us. When you don't pass one, it shows a lack of political will and conviction (lack of professional courage). When you don't follow one, it leaves us to pick up the mess and pay for the damage you have "unknowingly" done. When you overspend without one, it doesn't allow us to see who and where the extra money went and hold them accountable.

Current "Budget" is about 4.5 Trillion dollars, while GDP is about 14.3 Trillion.
Current "Budget" spends about 1.645 Trillion more than current revenue provides.
Current "Budget" didn't exist for over 2 ½ years.

Idea- We NEED to pass a law where a lack of a budget forces a national shutdown, without option. NO "continuing resolutions". That would force all politicians to the table to deal with each other. My take is that people are either part of the solution or part of the problem. Until we get politicians to deal with each other, and to deal for the American peoples best interest and long term success- they are part of the problem(not them, but the inherent weakness of politicians in general). Until they are forced to come to the table and resolve issues, they will not do so.

Side Note-   The New York Times posted an interesting challenge about how YOU would choose to Balance to Budget. Here is the link:
http://www.nytimes.com/interactive/2010/11/13/weekinreview/deficits-graphic.html

The lack of political accountability and direct urgent problem resolution is the tragic heart of the matter.

Revenue- Tax base, Deductions, and new sources

We are suffering under the burden of too many taxes, too many surcharges, too many ways of the government reaching into our pockets and taking our money. We are suffering in a society where the rich do not pay enough because they can legally work out of it, the lower income do not pay as they have no money to give, yet the backs of the working middle class (as defined by each locality since money in the Midwest goes much further than money in the cities of say Boston or NY as an example).

The solution is one of Timing. When the economy went south in 2008, Arizona almost immediately put legislation through that would increase taxes for the next 3 years to get them back where they needed to be. My point is that everyone in Arizona was put in a position to pay a little more of their share TEMPORARILY to get out of a bad spot. Yes- they shouldn't have been in that spot to begin with, but I do not look at life through perfect "hindsight" adjusted goggles- I look at life through a series of lenses which take philosophy, reality, 'do-ability', and fairness all into consideration. What Arizona did was confront the reality they faced quickly (getting ahead of the issue), fairly (all paid into it), within their agreed philosophy and obviously do-able from the citizens end as they elected this as the best course of action.

The Timing and Solution is best looked at from a broad scope and then dialed back into specifics. Today and going forward for about 18 years- the US Government will be put under tremendous financial pressure and pain as the baby-boomers retire and start getting all the social services they are "entitled" to as currently written. This will cost us Trillions we do not have. Period. Anyone trying to argue otherwise is silly. This needs to be dealt with now. Anyone trying to argue otherwise is even sillier. This will not go away, nor is it debatable. That is the silliest thought under the sun. Hope is not a solution in itself.

The Solution will be one that combines a current reality based combination of tax changes and deep spending cuts(defined by me as spending less than last year, not less than the anticipated increase which is the current Gov't game) with a long term picture of where to end up. To put it differently, IF you offered the US taxpayer a fair and balanced approach, giving them an increase now for a definitive reduction and simplification in say 10-15 years- they would accept it. Once the Boomers are into and mostly passed their drawdown of services, then the burden becomes much more manageable. BUT that cannot mean go back to spending widely or blindly, it would need to be kept in check while relieving the saddle of tax burdens, both the increase implemented temporarily and the multitude of various taxes now that punish the middle class. Reduce, simplify, eliminate becomes the mantra of our future when it comes to the revenue side of the equation.

Idea- Why not make a deal with all the overseas profits by US businesses? The number being tossed around is about 2 Trillion dollars in money looking to be repatriated back to the US. Instead of taxing those corporations 35% to bring it home- why not make it 17.5%? Take 10% in true taxes, 5% as a "start up fee" send _directly to the SBA_, and earmark 2.5% to be spent by a mandated date on large capital expenditures by their own company above and beyond what they currently spend? This would inject roughly 200 Billion dollars as true tax money, provide 100 Billion in new business start up money (to drive small purchases and employment), and provide 50 Billion in additional spending on large Cap Ex.

Idea- Why not promote the Treasury SmartExchange program (buying of US Savings Bonds directly from the Treasury) more than now? Direct investment into future of America, gets a better return than when buying 10 year notes, electronically done and managed. IF you believe in America and believe in our future, why wouldn't you? How about take this current program to a new level and make it pre-tax to a certain level? But knowing about that program is critical. It is completely undersold to the American taxpayer because there is not vested interest in talking about it.

And last time I looked- money here in our economy is better than money outside our country in someone else's economy. Then repeat this process the year after only for those who participate this year, and only for those companies who maintain or add US jobs year-over-year.

Debt (total Nat'l amount owed), Deficit (annual spending over budget)

Spending money you do not have- it is as simple as that. Politicians have made careers out of spending money that wasn't there, that was not their own- now or ever, and benefitted personally by doing it. I do not have enough time on the planet to explain how much that bothers me- so I will save that rant. Suffice to say that this particular habit is the single biggest blight on our society as it pulls our resources blindly away from other things, impacts the value of our dollar, undermines our confidence, and puts our future in jeopardy. This irresponsible drawdown must stop, and the rate of spending must be radically reduced from current levels. I know- how do you reduce now without hurting our currently frail economy? So let's take it in steps.

The current arrangement cannot continue- agreed? So we need to temper spending, find add'l money where we can, and all get over our little piece of the pie that we will need to pay. But why should I pay more? Save it- since we have all benefitted directly or indirectly by the over-spending, we really can't argue when someone drops a small check on the table at the end of our dinner.

Eventually my answer is even simpler- IF in one of your pockets you had 20 dollars and instead of handing that to the government you could do anything you wanted- What would you do? Save it or spend it- right? Either one is a good thing for the economy so what did we would be better off- right? Giving the Government less is the eventual goal, as is choosing individually where our money goes.

Until then, the Revenue side must be temporarily increased as a bridge to our future, but the Spending side being reduced now slightly, and increasingly as time and demands play out is the crucial piece of the puzzle. Hear this- IF that doesn't happen, nothing else matters for the financial end will simply be written. That is not a possibility; it is a mathematical statement of fact. Where we cut is not as crucial as THAT we cut.

Flat tax? Fair tax? Progressive tax? National Sales Tax? Simplify the Tax code? Eliminate deductions? Broaden the base? HOW do we get the necessary money to continue until we can reduce spending safely? HOW do we reduce spending enough to not raise taxes at the worst possible economic time? Tough questions, to be sure, that need immediate and decisive action. Fix It Now, and let the new journey begin.

The Congress recently put together a "Super Committee" to come together and find a "smart" solution, to avoid the harsh mandated cuts which would be triggered by a lack of joint solution. Result- couldn't get it done. Think THAT through- they couldn't agree on finding 1.2 Trillion *OVER 10 YEARS* (simple math of 120

Billion a year), at a time when we need them to find 1.*645 Trillion a YEAR* to break even and several Trillion to get us out of this fiscal mess. THAT is the best they could do. This result takes me back to a simple belief- that *the only people who will actually DO THIS will be moderates who do not WANT the job.* Basically, a career extremist has 2 forces at work against them (either political end of the spectrum). First, they need to satisfy their base to get re-elected, which means don't compromise. Second, they want to be re-elected, which is a more powerful force to these selfish individuals than fixing the countries ills by thinking, deciding, and acting on our behalf. Doing what is "right and necessary" is never the same thing as what is "easiest and painless".

Idea- The only guarantee that our future politicians will not put us back in the same mess is a *Balanced Budget Amendment*. It should have some latitude from year to year, given we will have years we run a surplus and years we run a deficit based strictly on market fluctuations. That "give and take" needs strict parameters, predetermined priorities, and the overall package is one to be voted on by the American people. When it comes to a 15 Trillion dollar pile of debt, a run rate of 1.7 Trillion per year, and an economy of 14.3 Trillion overall in the balance- how could you not at least put it in front of the American people and let us decide?

Side note-   Remember an important piece of the economic riddle, the economic pace will pick back up, and with that comes an increase in the revenue stream. We can decrease the revenue rate to accelerate the economic rate, which in turn will increase the overall revenue stream. Also, when was the last time you heard the phrase or use of PAYGO (pay as you go)?

Small Business Administration (SBA)-

This is probably one of the least utilized and talked about programs during economic downturns. WHY! That wasn't a question, it was a total "I don't get that" moment.

The SBA (should be called the NEW Business Administration) is charged with helping new business development. With basically 80% of the jobs in America accounted for by small businesses, the value of the SBA is paramount to our success down than road and absolutely one of the critical steps toward solving our economic problems- job creation will start and end at this level. The SBA continues to develop future new businesses, mentor and support individuals with the economic spirit and resolve to start a new business, and see it gets funded and founded- even at a time when its economic resources have not been sufficiently expanded.

Idea- Remember the idea about repatriating profits from overseas? Remember the 100 Billion dollar injection to the SBA? My idea is to shove that liquidity away from random spending on other issues or pet projects and put it right in the hands of people dealing with Americans in need of startup capital. Think about it as the loan the banks can't or won't give. Think of it as the push that ideas need to become entities, before they can qualify for large venture capital (and all the associated strings that come with VC). Think about it as a way to renew hope in the dream of American capitalism.

Side note- With 100 Billion of new money injected, it would create 500,000 new businesses (assuming a startup loan of $200,000 on average). That would immediately employ 500,000 people as owners and assuming history repeats itself- they would employ approximately 4 additional people per business (historical average). The net gain for this 100 Billion of New Business injection would result in approximately 2.5 million new jobs in America.

New businesses get people off unemployment. New businesses hire about 4 people over the first couple years on average. New businesses buy things from existing businesses. New businesses pay taxes. New businesses are the engine of our economy.

New businesses become the ultimate solution for the ultimate problem- **JOBS in America**.

Health Care   --   Cost, Structure, Coverage

Although the Obama "Affordable Healthcare Act" plan is a huge horribly thought out mess which was politically successful and operationally a nightmare- let alone a possible legal overstep, the fact remains that the Health Care in America (as constructed) is broken or tremendously flawed.

The Cost of Health Care in the last decade has basically exploded, up several hundreds of percentage points. THIS is the piece which is killing the US citizen and business. THIS needs to be dealt with.

The Structure is another sticking point- we are a nation of states who have rights and legal controls, we are a capitalistic nation which does not decide for people, but allow them the Power to decide for themselves.

The Coverage is missing about 30-40 million people- no matter what your stance is- we need to address that, and fix the coverage so all can have access, we can control the cost and structure of it, plan and budget for it, as opposed to be held hostage to it as we currently are.

Idea- Why didn't we take the uncovered and roll them strategically into the Medicaid/Medicare system, ask them to pay a "fair" token amount plus co-pay for that, and then work with the Health Care facilities on using economy-of-scale to reduce pricing? Why aren't we leveraging the HUGE amount of Federal buying power into cost savings? Why aren't we pressuring the big Pharmaceutical companies into reducing American costs, and increasing the breaks they give other nations who pay far less than we do for the very same drugs?

Idea- Why not create incentives for healthy living? Give tax credits for living within a range of your ideal body weight to lessen obesity, same for non-smokers. What about mandating blood testing and MRIs every 2 years for all adults 30 years and older (all costs pre-covered by health care packages)? We would catch huge amounts of issues much earlier than we do (similar to annual pap and breast exams for women currently). And similarly, why don't we penalize people who fail to get these things done by paying a tax surcharge? Currently what happens is people wait until it is too late, then have high cost treatments, and we all have our rates go up to pay for it. Why aren't we ahead of the health care and cost curve as opposed to reacting to it (and being caught in the high end of it)?

Idea- Why don't we extend the exclusive rights of the big Pharmaceutical companies for drugs they create? IF someone invents a "gadget", they get rights forever through the patent office. IF someone writes a book, they get 50 years past the lifetime of the author. IF someone develops the "next best drug", they get 7 years- then everyone can copy it as generic and make money off their idea. Why? The R&D money was spent, and needs to be recouped. By getting them 3 extra years, they could amortize the costs over more years and price the drugs even cheaper. THIS idea, coupled with higher prices abroad and large purchasing power discounts under Medicaid and Medicare, would go a long way toward reducing costs of health care in the US.

Idea- My younger son was brought into this world by a wonderful physician who did what was right for my wife and child, and many more before them. The tragic part is he has literally stopped delivering babies- the rate increases of malpractice insurance just made it not worth his while (he would make more money NOT doing his craft). He gave up something he was good at, and something he loved doing- for all the wrong reasons. What about limiting malpractice awards to a sane dollar number ($5 Million maximum). No one wants doctors to get off scot-free, nor do you want incompetency even practicing medicine- you just cannot keep punishing good doctors with the broad stroke of "everyone could make a mistake". ALL doctors will make mistakes. They are human, not robots. They need to be put in a better position to succeed, not pushed out when they are good. How does our Health Care system get better by forcing out competent doctors for the wrong reasons based on the cost of insurance?

More questions, not enough answers- I get it. But my point is this, address the issue as opposed to get financially overwhelmed by it. Fix It. It would be a huge start toward fixing the broken social and financial piece within the fabric of our economy. NO- I do not think that the Obama plan is the right answer, but it was the right topic. Fix it- legally, economically, socially- within the framework of our capitalistic, free democratic republic. What was created recently will not work (cover 20 million add'l with no extra revenue, no change to structure, slight and forced change to cost containment, and no additional doctors to share that burden), nor were we educated on its "true" benefits (flaws) nearly enough.

Side note-   Fix it- of course. But ask yourself this simple question- When was the last time Government took something over and actually made it better and cheaper? My answer in my entire lifetime is "Never". So why would we commit 16% of our Gross Domestic Product to a system created to fail (that is also irreversible once truly implemented)?

For more information about how "Obama care" (The Affordable Health Care Act) actually works, please visit the below sight:

http://www.whitehouse.gov/healthreform/healthcare-overview#works

Oil/Energy- policy, dependency, refineries, and money lost

I could have combined this with the EPA rant, but I have a particular idea to toss out that I think would really work (several actually).

Idea- Change our current Gasoline Energy Tax from a set dollar amount to a percent, both at the federal and state level. Seems simple right? The idea is this- when the price of Oil went up to about $150 per barrel a few years ago, it took about 7 Trillion(yes, Trillion) dollars out of the economy. The price-per-barrel increase on our usage, plus the loss in that money cycling through our economy, is devastating. WOW- how we stayed afloat then is beyond me. But since we did, why not change it to a percent, so as the price went up we could keep money here-remember other revenues go down so this would help offset it.

Idea- Build refineries here in the US- the last was built in the 1970's and several have actually closed. As the US Gov't has military bases throughout the country, my idea is simple. Build, with the help of private money and technology, current and state-of-the-art facilities on several of these bases. It would keep the bases operating, give them something to protect in this current geo-political climate, create thousands of high paying jobs (let alone the construction jobs initially), eliminate the "not in my backyard" argument and allow us to refine more cheaply and cleanly the oil we need. Control is key in this battle for energy independence.

Idea- What about eliminating the 87 octane gasoline at the pump? It would allow refiners to maximize profits making less types of gas, it would help improve gas mileage, and it would help carbon emissions.

Idea- What about setting an annual increase in a cars minimal MPG? IF it underperforms, the model gets hit with a tax surcharge at purchase (and at every tax filing during ownership of that model). Think it through- the people who drive low mileage vehicles are putting pressure on all of us by using more gas/oil. This increased demand (unnecessarily) increases the price at the pump. The use of tax surcharges simply asked the ones with poor behavior to pay their fair share and lighten the load on the rest of us. And vice-versa, what about tax credits for people whose primary car is a top-end MPG vehicle? Punish the bad, reward the good- what is more American than that?

Idea- The single largest purchaser in the world is probably the US Gov't- so why don't they get the most bangs for our buck? Why aren't they leveraging that purchasing power into savings for the US taxpayer? My idea would be to buy very high mileage vehicles as part the US fleet. Why wouldn't our tax dollars benefit by buying electric cars, using less fuel, and lowering the cost of eco-friendly vehicles in the process? Also- think about the reduction in fuel demand and the impact that would have on oil and gas prices. Also- think about how technology needs to be embraced to save our money in other ways- put GPS on these cars and track where and how they are used. Government vehicles should be for government use- not personal cars for personal use *at the price of the American taxpayer*.

Idea- You know what got me about the entire BP oil fiasco? A couple days later Venezuela had a leak, yet shut it off with remote sensors and had no damage. Really? I have always considered America the best country in the world (since Super-powers should lead by example) and we should always be the best at everything. We should spend the extra dollars to have the best safety equipment, not in hindsight- but because that is how we build things. Every remote sensor (for offshore deep water drilling controls) costs about $500,000, which on the balance sheets of oil companies is peanuts.

IF you don't like the ideas, come up with a better one. But simply, something needs to be done.

Social Security

The Widows and Orphans program started in the early 1930's has morphed over the last approximately 80 years into a retirement entitlement for all Americans. It has been changed so many times over the years that I literally lost track.

Here is what you need to know- NO ONE ever pays in enough for what they take out. NO ONE is legally entitled to this; it could be changed or stopped at any time- without recourse. NO ONE has the political will to stop it. Picture it as a huge boulder tumbling down a mountain-side. Would you stand in front of it, even it was heading toward a village to do damage? You get my political point. The reality is we cannot afford the current system and we cannot do away with the current system. So what now?

IF you believe that the current system, although flawed and mathematically devastating, should stay- then we need to make some structural changes. First, uncap the contribution level(current cap is $106,800) like Medicare was back in 1993 so that no matter how much you make Social Security gets paid its percentage from the employee and employer all the way up the income scale. Raise the age requirement for full benefits to age 70, eliminate or minimize the COLA (cost of living adjustments), and call it a day. And then go cut aggressively in another area.

IF you believe that the current system cannot stay, since it is overwhelming our financial resources and built on the premise of a growing population base- then we need to replace it. Remember- no one besides the truly wealthy are financially able to handle the burden of retirement costs. Most Americans NEED this Social Security money much more than they WANT it. Without it, they could not make ends meet for as long as they live, with all the other tedious and ever rising costs that come with age like health care in general, pharmaceuticals in specific, commodities pushing oil/gas/food products higher still, long term home health services, etc.

Want to get some idea of how out of control the costs have been handled and increased?

Back in 1981 the program covered about 36 M people, had an earned income cap of $29,700 and cost a total of $126.695 billion. Since then, the programs benefit payout per month has increased by 300%.

Then in 1985, the program covered about 37 M people, had an earned income cap of $39,600 and cost a total of $171.150 billion. Since then, the program benefit payout per month has increased by 200%.

In 1993, the coverage expanded to 42 M people, had an earned income cap at $57,600, and a total cost of $273.104 billion. Since then, the program benefit payout has doubled.

Recently, the program covered 53M people, had an earned income cap at $106,800 and cost $516.192 billion. With boomers retiring, the costs just explode.

Idea- The premise is based on the origin of Social Security when created. IT was designed for the people who could not take care of themselves, not as a blanket retirement perk for all Americans. Having said that- the new model would involve a tier system of ages to receive corresponding benefits. The First tier would be ages 60 and above. They would receive partial benefits at age 60 and full benefits at age 70. My definition of partial would be 50% of full, not the current 25-30% reduction in benefits. They would receive the current maximum benefit, but would not receive any COLA (cost of living adjustment) ever. The Second tier would be ages 45-59. They would receive partial benefits at age 60 and full benefits at age 65. The new full benefit level would be 15% less than now, and partial would be half of that. This would be a fixed benefit and only be increased by a set 1% COLA. The Final tier would be age 44 and under. They would receive partial benefits at age 55 and full benefits at age 60. Their benefit level would be 15% less than the second tier, and partial would be half of that amount. This would be a fixed benefit and only be increased by a set 1% COLA. The Second and Final tier would receive a minimal COLA (say 1% a year) on Full Benefits only. ****Critical to this idea** is also 3 qualifiers- you could not receive SS benefits while 1) fully employed   2) having a Net Worth higher than $500,000 excluding primary residence or 3) making more than $40,000 per year in total income (earned or unearned). The point of these qualifiers is to get the money to those who NEED it, not to those who are "ENTITLED" to it. The people who have enough would retire earlier, opening up employment opportunities. People who didn't immediately qualify would qualify eventually as their wealth or income diminished, or they retired (some minimal part time work would still be allowed). Also, the total "credits" needed to qualify for benefits needs to be radically raised. The current figure of 40 credits (takes about 10-12 years of full employment to hit that) is far too low. We should raise that level to about 60-70 credits, keeping people employed longer to qualify for full benefits. Anyone not reaching that level would still receive partial benefits after hitting a lower threshold. Lastly, uncapping the contribution level from the current $106,800 level to unlimited (similar to Medicare in 1993) and opening up additional legal contributions to 401K(and IRAs) for the Second and Final tiers would help offset the lower benefit stream they would receive.

Example- A person is age 60 or above now- they would receive their check of say $900 (partial) or $1800 a month (full) for life. But it would never increase. The current system might increase that by 2-3% each year. The 2% each year (potential) is about $384/yr for every individual in the system. They would start partial benefits at the age of 60 or full benefits at age 70. They would receive benefits only if not fully employed, net worth was less than 500K, and they had an income of less than 40K annually.

A person who is age 45-59 now, would be eligible for partial benefits at age 60 and full benefits at age 65 – 15% less than the First tier, so benefits would be $765 for partial and $1530 for full. But remember, each person would collect from age 65 (two years earlier than current), have a greater legal contribution level into 401K and IRAs, and receive a minimal COLA of 1% on full benefits a year. The same qualifiers would exist about employment, net worth, and income level.

A person who is in the Final tier of under age 45 would get $650 partial benefit and a $1300 full benefit (15% less than the Second tier). BUT remember, they would collect partial at age 55 and full at age 60. This tier would have the ability to contribute more to 401K (and IRAs) under law, get a 1% COLA each year on full benefits, and not have to meet the net worth or income criteria- although they still would not receive benefits as long as they were fully employed. This Tier and all who follow it would need to hit the raised credit level of approximately 60 to qualify for full benefits, anyone who hit the current 40 credit mark would receive only partial benefits. The Final tier would also be the new "standard" benefit.

Side note- Remember raising the 401K (and IRA) limits? Why not tie that in to the "age" tier system of Social Security. IF someone is going to receive less benefit from SS, then it only stands to reason they will need to fund their retirement some other way. By making this option available, it would help solve for everyone's benefit.

Side note- Another huge advantage of dropping the qualifying age for Social Security is that some people might choose to stop working earlier, and this would have a positive impact on unemployment as the natural attrition would provide job opportunities for the unemployed and upward mobility for some currently deadlocked in a career by someone above them who cannot, or chooses not to, retire.

Side note-   The numbers above *do not* include the Disability portion of the benefit program. Something worth noting and looking into the validity of would be the recent jump in Disability claims and benefit payments. The number of claims and payments has jumped from a 1981 number of about $16 billion, 1985 numbers of $19 billion, 1993 number of $31 billion, to a 2008 number of $109 billion. See the jump?

Website:
Social Security Administration (SSA)
Contact via the Web:
Contact the Social Security Administration (SSA)
Contact In-Person:
Find an Office Near You

Medicaid- Health Coverage for the Poor

No one should ever kick someone when they are down, so this Healthcare Coverage for Low Income people makes a lot of sense. How can you have people completely at risk to major health issues, not provide something for them, and yet consider yourself to still be human? NO- that doesn't mean they should get a free ride. One of the commercials that stands out is for a scooter for people to ride around on in their home, mall, etc- the point is that if you cannot afford it, they are covered by a *completely* by a government plan. Really? Why?

The point should be that everyone should have a "deductable", or a level of financial commitment to whatever it is they receive. It doesn't matter whether it is $20 to a scooter, $5 to a doctor, $1 to a prescription- no one gets anything for free. Unfair? Go get a better offer somewhere else.

Whatever the current contributions, the level needs to be increased over time slightly. Again, it simply is keeping pace with the level of drain this puts on the American budget and economy as other people need to pay for this service. Make no mistake, the people receiving this do not deserve it or have they earned it, they are simply in hard times or don't have enough income to make it all work in their life. Helping them as they are in this spot is fine, but it needs to come with a price.

They need to be educated about preventive medicine. They need to be educated about nutrition. They need to have and go regularly to a doctor to catch things earlier. They need to be incentivized into going to cheaper doctors than an Emergency Room for simple things. They need to understand the repercussions for their decisions and be held somewhat accountable.

Idea- What about providing a set dollar amount in coverage a year and if you could spend less than that, and do some simple preventative things like not smoke, stay within a modest weight range, etc- you would get an annual reward(whether a one-time true check or a tax credit to ensure a rebate). Remember right now this is a drain on our budget, and there is no reason for these individuals to change. THAT needs to be a focus of debate, not with them as victims or villains- but with them as a piece of our new reality that needs to be dealt with fairly and compassionately.

Idea- One of the most critical ideas about solving the Medicaid and Medicare involves the purchasing of pharmaceuticals (prescription drugs). The US Gov't should use their intense size and reach to broker deals with the Pharmaceutical companies which lower the cost of drugs. The Bush Administration actually gave away this leverage, again a sign of our governments misguided focus on the wrong things (not protecting and benefitting the American taxpayer) based on the wrong priorities (usually their donors).

The days of free rides need to end, since we now live in the land of tough choices. I will be asked to pay more in taxes or give something up, just a matter of time. Why? The answer is simple- we cannot afford to keep going down this exact path. Change is coming. The only fuzzy part is what exactly the new norm will look like.

Website:
Medicaid and CHIP Payment and Access Commission
E-mail:
webmaster@macpac.gov
Address:
1800 M Street, NW
Suite 350N
Washington, DC 20036
Phone Number:
202-273-2460

Medicare- Health Coverage for the Elderly

Health care for the elderly is second only to Social Security in its financial burden it is about to put on the American economy in the coming decades. The baby-boomer generation, coupled with the ever rising health care costs, will be retiring and losing employer sponsored health care soon. As the largest generation by population starts using federal programs such as Social Security and Medicare, the burden will be in the Trillions not Billions. So these two issues cannot be left untouched, nor can they be eliminated. They need to be reasonably confronted with compassion.

Medicare is under tremendous cost pressures. In my opinion, we need to start at the very beginning. What players are involved and how can they help? Doctors get a set fee, but what restrictions are they under? What tests are given as a way of speeding patients away or protecting the doctors' judgment as opposed to what is needed? What drugs are used and are they the cheapest best choice? Do patients go to the Emergency room or are they educated on using their primary care physician?

The concern I have for Medicare overall is an odd one based on the time we live in. When the Affordable Health Care Act goes into full effect it will push an additional 20 million into coverage, yet the number of doctors in the US has not gone up to account for it. Have you been to the doctor lately? I had an appointment and when I showed up 10 minutes early, did my paperwork- I still had to wait 1 hr to be seen. Does that sound like a doctor who is underutilized and lush with free time? Do you see the amount of doctors who accept Medicare/Medicaid going up or down once you push 20 million add'l patients into the global waiting room?

We need changes. We need compassion. We need foresight.

Contact Medicare

The Centers for Medicare & Medicaid Services (CMS), a branch of the U.S. Department of Health and Human Services, is the Federal agency that administers the Medicare program and monitors the Medicaid programs offered by each state.

Medicare makes it easy for you to get information. You can find answers to general questions about eligibility, coverage, and Medicare Summary Notices (MSNs) on this Web site. You can also compare health and drug plans, Medigap policies, hospitals, nursing homes, and more!

For specific questions about your claims, medical records, or expenses, visit MyMedicare.gov, or call 1-800-MEDICARE.

For more specific contact information, see Where to Get Your Medicare Questions Answered.

If you want someone to be able to call 1-800-MEDICARE on your behalf, you need to fill out a "Medicare Authorization to Disclose Personal Health Information" form so Medicare can give your personal health information to someone other than you.

Mailing Address
Centers for Medicare & Medicaid Services
7500 Security Boulevard
Baltimore MD 21244-1850

The Federal Reserve-

Love it or hate it- it is a piece of our financial institutions and always will be. Agree with it or not, it has a duel mandate of low employment and contained inflation. They are a non-transparent quasi private agency that makes many nervous or worse. The Fed is run by a rotating Board of Governors, headed by the Chairman. They run regions canvassing the US and control all the banks and lending institutions within that region. They work with Treasury, and at the behest of the Presidency.

A critical piece about the Fed- they are not able to do it alone. So for good or for bad, they should not get the credit or the blame entirely. They can be a piece of the solution- but not a solution by itself. The policy they follow should mirror that of the US Gov't. The policy they set should be focused exclusively on the US and exclusively on the needs of their mandates. Period. Those countries of the world need their backing, need their comments, or that the Fed wants to get involved should never happen- no matter how good the premise would be of WHY they would want to do that.

Idea- Make what they do and what they could do much more transparent than it currently is. Where do they have their money? How big is their balance sheet? What options are on the table or could be? Who holds them accountable and how?

Idea- Make the tiers of regional banks underneath the Fed abide by the policy directions given out. Why would the Fed be in charge of spurring job growth, but not be able to push new business development lending at the lower levels of banking? Why would banks be able to sit on huge amounts of capital, benefit by the lending spreads to their profitability, without actually doing real banking activities? The primary focus should be in supporting new business and capital expenditure outlays; with the understanding they make smart strategic safe loans within the parameters of the time.

Side note- Several groups are carrying on about the gold standard. Bring it back. Why? And more importantly, How? Have you seen the price of gold? Imagine if you will that the dollar was pegged to it. WOW! Who controls the commodities markets? Speculators- people who are short term driving a tight market by injecting huge amounts of money and using geo-political events to exaggerate the move. THAT is who you want controlling the value of our dollar? That seems more like the tail wagging the dog.

Housing

WOW- what a tough last 4 years in housing, the last three in a recession-like economy (if not a Great Recession like it felt). Foreclosures, people in homes "underwater"(owing more than the home is worth), ghost inventories, people in default, government programs which didn't work, robo-signing by banks which are impersonal enough, government officials pointing fingers at everyone except themselves, etc.

That we HAVE a housing market is saying something. That it is in disarray still says even more. That we haven't found a true balance or a way out of these inventories/foreclosures speaks to a lack of ideas and leadership. That we are all over the map speaks to the fact there are too many hands in the pie for the markets to behave like the self-cleansing mechanisms that they are- part for good reasons, part for bad.

The good news about people getting in the way of true market mechanics is that home prices are higher now than they should be- period.

The bad news about people getting in the way of true market mechanics is that uncertainty is much higher that it should be- period.

The unfortunate thing is they both go hand-in-hand. Let the markets fall and it would be short term painful, but long term certain. Prop the markets up buys time, but at the unrelenting price called uncertainty. I have a different direction for us to take.

Idea- The government (yes, I said it) could actually do some good- either directly or indirectly. They need to mandate the demolition of some of the housing glut. That is right- tear them down literally. By removing excess inventory (say 1 in 20 on banks books) the housing prices would stabilize at current or higher levels. The inventories would need to be accounted for, so as not to impact banks capitalization overall. The demolition could be considered an anti-infrastructure play. It would create demolition jobs, help home prices(start to relieve some pressure on underwater homes sooner), eventually create new jobs in construction at a much sooner point in time, remove some blights in neighborhoods(condemned buildings, vandalized homes, eyesores which are unkempt, etc.), and create tremendous certainty earlier in time moving forward.

Remember- we are in a time of a 'new normal', where the economy will not grow as quick as it has historically, where homes will be unloaded by boomers more so going forward- not less, where there are less home buyers coming into the market than are leaving, where most former home owners will not qualify for a mortgage for some time to come.

Idea- What about a one year moratorium on NEW home construction? You could buy a home and remodel, or you could wait (maybe pay a one-time surcharge)? The point would be this. With enough homes on the market and then some, why would we allow more homes to be built at a time when we cannot support the current home price as is? Why not make them pay-up for it OR not do it? If the argument is we would lose construction jobs, then who would do the remodeling? The sooner we settle out home prices, the sooner we can return to "normal" and the sooner REAL construction pricing and jobs return. My cousin (who has done construction on the West coast for 20 plus years says he doesn't see construction coming back for a long time- 10 years was his number).

Side note- We will come to a point where we will need to forgive the current credit issues at a pace unheard of in history. Just planting that seed now, but it will be part of the ultimate solution. And yes, it means the very people who overstretched before and helped create this mess will benefit earlier than they should. Get over it; I have- since we will need them involved productively in our society as consumers and home owners to make it all work.

Freddie Mac and Fannie Mae- Housing Mortgage GSEs

Be careful what you wish for- you just might get it.
But I'll get back to that...

The honest truth prior to the economic collapse is that everyone wanted everyone else to have a home, whether they could afford it or not. So most people got into situations they couldn't handle if these went south (as they always do eventually). The main vehicles for mass destruction were Freddie Mac and Fannie Mae. These GSE's (Government Sponsored Entities) were handling about 90% of the mortgage business in the US at a time when the mortgage business (and the repackaging of CDUs and Swaps) were the rage of profitability on Wall Street. Then obviously the economic collapse of 2008 happened, the term Too Big to Fail was created, and we started in to rebuild our economy. One of the many reassurances to come spinning out of Congress was Dodd-Frank. It is the simplified name for the financial oversight law passed by Congress. It is a huge document covering almost every aspect of the financial services industries- to protect us from this ever happening again. Wait- did I say almost?

Almost means that Freddie and Fannie were exempt- as in left out of being re-regulated. Let me say if again- the two entities with the most mortgage exposure was exempt from oversight. As of now, they have taken more than 150 Billion in bailout funds, hold 95% of the home mortgage exposure in the US, and have been taken over by the US government.

There is only one thing left to do. Deal with them. How do you make 95% of the mortgage market go away? How do you break up GSEs? How do you bailout multi-trillion dollar institutions? The current winds are blowing toward privatize. That's what most people are hoping and wishing for?

Remember what I said? Be careful what you wish for- you just might get it. For the people wanting to privatize- what happens down the road when someone wants a mortgage? IF private, then it is in the hands of the market. But we talked about how Government hasn't handled too big to fail, how they allow things to get out of control, and in the case of "It's a Wonderful Life"- remember Mr. Potter, the banker, and how he controlled everything? Do we truly want the biggest banks in the country or world handling all the mortgages and holding that over our heads? And you think they were too big to fail now? Picture those very banks taking on a few trillion dollars in mortgage steroids.

I do not usually say this, but sometimes you should leave well enough alone. Just clean them up over time and then make the Congress, oversight panel, and regulators do their jobs and keep it where it should be and not overextend.

Idea- Since the Government keeps coming up with ideas to help people almost in foreclosure, people underwater, people about to default- which rewards the bad timing/bad decisions/hard luck of their life, I have a different thought. Why not make a onetime "refinancing" available to ALL Americans? This would help those in need, and not penalize those who are still OK. It would help with liquidity at the household level and allow for higher spending (helping economy) or higher savings (helping banks capitalization requirements and loan availability). Right now, the banks get to "make money" on the increased spread between old loans and new lower lending rate from the Fed.

Sallie Mae- Student Loan GSE

Riddle- How do you get more people into college when not all of them should be there? Unfortunately, that is the state of education in America. You need a degree to get a "real" job, which means that a lot of people who shouldn't be in college actually end up there- and Sallie Mae (Student Loan GSE facility) is happy to loan them the money. After graduation, you get a job and can spend the next two decades paying it off. But wait a second- who says you get a job right away out of college (current dilemma)? Why should everyone have to go to college to get a "real" job? And why are our colleges taking anyone with a checkbook into higher education?

Sallie Mae was created long ago to make school affordable to more people. Now, higher learning takes more money than to buy a starter house. Because of that, two issues arise. First, doesn't it kind of defeat the purpose to get an education when you spend a huge chunk of your life under the burden of paying it off? Secondly, WHY does it cost so much to get an education to begin with? The answer to that is funny- because so much demand is there. What? Yes- you got it. IF less people actually went to college, the lack of demand would force schools to charge less to increase enrollment. So the very lunacy of having to have a degree to get a job is propping up the price of higher learning and making people go *who shouldn't even qualify academically if the standards were higher*.

I am not of the opinion that every child should go to college. I do agree that every kid should pick a path forward in life. That doesn't mean ALL children should go to college. It means each case is different, both for the child and the needs of society going forward.

Idea- What about raising the value of trade schools or entrepreneurship? Whatever happened to apprenticeships? What about increasing the breadth of military recruiting to increase the talent of all branches and give young adults a time to settle out on what they want from life (none of us truly knew at 18 years old what we wanted to do for the rest of our life)?

Federal Deposit Insurance Corp. (FDIC)

One of the best adjustments during the recent economic collapse was the increase in Federal Deposit Insurance per account. The amount was raised from $100,000 to $250,000 per account. What does that do? It calms the big money accounts down and prevent the biggest run on banks, which in turn would destroy banks capitalization, which was one of the primary drivers of the collapse- the lack of proper loan-to-capital ratios.

Quick point- when banks make a loan it is an Asset, when they take a deposit it is a Liability. It is the reverse for all business and people like you and me. It is in their best interest to maximize the loans over the deposits, but at some point the lack of deposits versus the totality of loans (and quality of those loans) becomes a precursor to disaster.

Picture a boulder on top of a hill, overlooking a town. At some point, the ground softens due to rain, and the boulder comes rushing toward the town and people hate living in that town at that moment- but right up until then, people loved living in that town a lot.

Timing is everything might apply, but it also has to do with good solid decision making based in reality. Can people afford to truly carry the mortgage? IF they can't what pressure will that put on the lending institution?

If the FDIC hadn't increased this level, we would have experienced more pressure on the banks at the worst possible time.

Website:
Federal Deposit Insurance Corporation (FDIC)
Contact via the Web:
Contact the Federal Deposit Insurance Corporation (FDIC)
Address:
Consumer Response Center
1100 Walnut St., Box #11
Kansas City, MO 64106

Military

Our military is one of the few things we all agree that the US Gov't should be doing for us, although the size and mandate is up for discussion daily. The military personnel are one of the greatest assets (and most underutilized) in our country. The goal is to keep America safe, not to be the police for the world at our expense. IF we intervene for our national safety, that is on us. IF the world needs our help to "police" a situation (recently Libya as an example), why would ALL costs be paid by that country or the countries needing our help? In this case, we don't use the oil Libya provides- Europe does. So, my mindset is for them to pick up the check or go it alone. I am not campaigning for Isolationism, just for us not to spend money we do not have, especially for other peoples' gain and agenda.

Idea- We should revamp the recruitment process, size and scope, individual capabilities/talent, and possibly consider a 2 year national mandated program for all Americans at 18 years of age. It would not be a combat oriented program, but an introduction to the military culture, training, systems, discipline, physicality, and opportunities of all branches. Each person would rotate through a 4 month program or each branch (Army, Navy, Marine, Air Force, Coast Guard) - then finish with a 4 month stint in the branch of their choice (priority based on level of individual performance. THIS is where the recruiters would spend the bulk of their time- since these people have performed well, have chosen that specific branch, and are a known quantity based on performance evaluations from all services. Our future military service would benefit, Americans would benefit, and our national pride and security would benefit.

Idea- Why not hire all future police, fire, EMT based on prior military training? Basically they are predetermined to understand chain of command, understand right vs. wrong, understand the need for discipline and loyalty. Isn't that who we want? Granted not every soldier would make a good cop- but why not take the ones that would as a priority first, then offset that with secondary hiring? It would be a huge reward for having served your country. It would be a huge recruiting tool going forward if this was known. It would benefit communities who need to hire and reduce overtime which is killing local budgets both in pay and benefits.

Environmental Protection Agency (EPA)

IF I hear of one more little lizard stopping an entire state from doing something, I think I will scream. Not very mature, I know- but seriously? I get the need to protect our Earth, after all it is the only one we will ever have. So there needs to be a focus on not destroying it- I grant that. My take is simple- do not tell me why I cannot do something without telling how I CAN do it. Be a part of the solution for a change. I recently listened to someone talk about the Keystone Pipeline from the environmental side. Her take was simply that the type of "dirty oil" is not something that should be allowed to be used in our country. OK- fine. So let me get this right- we will tell Canada "No thanks", they will ship it overseas, we will then import more oil than we would have to(possibly even bring this particular oil back in at a much more expensive rate) and let another country burn this cheaper full? So the dirty oil still affects our planet, and we get stuck holding the figurative check- again.

My analogy is simple- remember when you went to school and the teacher would talk bad about the kids who weren't there or the kids who were always late (before they arrived)? Shouldn't' the teacher call and talk to the parents of those who were NOT in class? Shouldn't the teacher deal with the LATE students? The kids, who are on time and in class should be REWARDED, not chastised. When it comes to carbon use, until there is a global initiative- it is worse than ridiculous to say NO to this cheaper oil. We could benefit and keep it out of others hands; we could use our savings to research new ways to refine to save our planet, to support other technologies. Today- we literally do the opposite.

Idea- I would suggest that the EPA makes suggestions about how to do things more eco-friendly. Be the leader, instead of the nay-sayor. IF you want a pipeline or want to drill offshore- the EPA should show how best to change your recommendations to help fit what are in the best interests of the US. THAT is becoming part of the solution, not part of the problem. You cannot stand in front of America and say "don't use oil" since our world would stop- literally. You also cannot look the other way as companies blatantly destroy the planet- the truth is in the middle and in working together. We all need to provide solutions, based in reality and within budgets, as part of a national plan of what is best for the country. As an example, we should help to reduce or eliminate foreign oil use, but at what price? But to just say NO simply penalizes the wrong people, sends a futile message, kills jobs and true competitiveness, and is not part of a cohesive overview that builds for a better tomorrow. This is also true for all other environmental topics.

Unions

Collusion, illegal as defined by Webster, is basically when Businesses get together to oppress Workers. I completely agree since true competition for labor talent is when the marketplace works best.

So riddle me this batman? Why are Unions even legal? I understand why they originated, but how can you argue that they are good for anyone today? They cost the members money, they cost the businesses money, they make labor more costly by doing this which is passed through to the consumer in the form of higher prices, they gain nothing by doing this in productivity, and they are the collective body of talent holding out against business unless their terms are met (whether peaceful or by protest). Then why?

Maybe someone can explain that to me one day.

Idea- What about a *"Right to Work"* national initiative? Why should we allow labor to hold business hostage? Why not let them have a venue to get fair wages and affordable benefits, but not at the price of losing our competitive advantage, and therefore pushing jobs overseas for all the wrong reasons? The best idea is when Companies and Labor meet in the middle and do what is best for the business- not what is best for one party or the other. In good times, all should benefit. In tough times, all must be willing to give something up. When someone does something bad, they should be held accountable. When someone is not as productive they should be dealt with, not lost based on lack of seniority.

Idea- IF Unions are part of the solution, not part of the problem- why don't they self-police? IF a member does something which threatens the company and labor (drinking on the job as an example), why wouldn't the Union deal with it? IF a member is underproductive, why wouldn't the Union deal with it and retrain or remove them for everyone's' benefit? Currently, the opposite is true- the stronger the Union the more security you have, and that translates into poor habits and behaviors in the workplace.

Side Note- This would include ALL government jobs as well. At what point did a Government job become an easier, more secure and more rewarding career path? It is my belief that all jobs should be paid fairly for its time, all jobs should have a route toward retirement which is contributed to, all jobs should have a benefits package which can be paid for in the future, not just a burden on society.

Pensions

Stick a fork in them they are done- they are another thing that was never thought through many years ago. How do you pay for current now, with a promise of money down the road as well? Then down the road actually have the money to pay for it? You end up paying the "new" employees more, the old employees more, and as your business/entity "succeeds"- you get stuck with a growing pile of labor benefits for people who no longer even produce a single thing for you. That 'success" is not success at all; it is a recipe for non-competitiveness. It needs to go away quickly as a piece of reworking the social and financial fabric that is today's America.

Idea- Educate all high school students on the *time value* of money. Incentivize all Americans to get into 401K's much earlier than they do. Drop the entry age from 21 to 16 years old. Why not? This only promotes savings earlier, allows them to lower their tax burden, and starts engraining best practices at an early age. The upside is huge and there isn't a downside.

Idea- STOP paying overtime- period. Why would you consciously under-employ, pay overtime(by design) which is a waste of money, use that as part of pension calculations, and then be on the hook for even more money that you don't have. The goal should be to *HIRE PEOPLE*, lower overtime to zero, pay fairly and within budget, lessen the cost burden of waste, and to get away from pensions and move to a 401K with matching situation.

Idea- Raise the annual amount both in percent and real dollars that one can contribute to 401Ks. Why not? You get social security tax now anyway, you maximize bank capitalization which allows them to loan, you build an inherent umbrella of safety for all who participate faster and confidence goes up. So again, why not?

Side note- Just a thought- we need to revisit the 20 year retirement time frame for things like military and police. That quicker turn around loses veterans, costs additional benefits for life longer, and hasn't been adjusted for the longer mortality rate we all now enjoy. If people live longer and additional moneys are now being spent on the back end- isn't it worth talking about moving the retirement time frame from 20 to 25 years (as an example)?

Immigration

The Immigration issue is not one single issue, but a series of decisions, actions, and policies to build for a better future. No matter what side of the political spectrum you fall on, that is a simple common ground of agreement. So let's deal with this in a series of discussions.

The first is a fairly simple one- legal vs. illegal immigration. Most people who come here legally, through proper channels, or/and are brought in for their specific set of skills or education are not the discussion. It is a painfully long and costly process, which is a separate issue since it increases the likelihood of someone choosing an illegal avenue. Also, the illegal avenue- although might be most commonly seen as a "build a wall" Hispanic issue, that is not the case. There are people coming in via boat, across from Canada, or across the Mexican border who are not Hispanic but simply using that route as a path of entry.

Second, the rate or access of illegal immigration is a more simple decision- build the wall to completeness, put troops or technology in place to patrol, use diplomacy to increase Mexico's legitimate help on their side of the border, involve military personnel- DHS technology and multi-government intelligence coordinated input. Remember, as you do this it will put tremendous strain on several industries that currently use (knowingly or unknowingly) illegal immigrants. The cost of what those industries put out *WILL* go up- you will pay more for landscaping, more for food in restaurants, more for produce and textiles, etc. - Period. Also, the jobs these people do are, for the most part, not jobs typical Americans have or would want. Would you want to be the cheap manual labor? Would you want to be the low man (woman) in the food chain? They do it because it is a step up from where they come from. Americans would do it as a step down based on what they know as normal.

Third, what do you do with the current illegal immigrants in America? Amnesty- do you reward illegal behavior? They currently get benefits like schooling and health care which drains our public funds. Deport them- that would cause a witch hunt of people based on profile or "tips" to law enforcement. Cut off their benefits? Is there the political will (you know how much courage our "leaders" have) to get this done if we believe it to be the best choice?

Fourth, the Federal Government is responsible for the policing of immigration- Period. The fact, that they do not enforce and represent us, does not give states the right to be creative with immigration policy on their own. The States should sue the US Government and force their hands through the courts. This is not a choice to implement but a need to protect our culture, our costs, and our safety (both nationally on a Terrorism level, and on a local crime basis). This is another failure in leadership.

Fifth, once we stop the "cheap labor" coming into our country, we will need to account for that dynamic shift in how we value labor and inflation. Think about the total upward shift on labor costs and the need to produce at a level to protect margins, this would be a major skew in time on how we track labor, cost increase metrics, and fight for cheap labor.

Idea- Amnesty, with a twist, is the best policy. Not because it rewards bad behavior (although that would happen incidentally), but the simple truth is these people currently fill a role in our culture or fabric of society. We cannot tear it apart without hurting surrounding pieces of that culture. The best solution I can think of is to streamline a way to get them legally into our culture, let them pay for the benefits they receive, expect them to behave in the mainstream of our society, and penalize them with loss of citizenship for failing to stay in that norm. If someone who is illegal becomes legal, why can't we put a "lien" on that status that holds them accountable for their behaviors? IF they behave illegally (felony convictions), don't prosecute sentence to jail time- revoke their status and deport them. Even a temporary lien (say 5-10 years), this would balance the equation of rewarding the bad behavior of coming here illegally with the incentive to have solid habits that support our culture without the pain of tearing them out of the fabric of society.

Side note-   this will never go away. No matter what steps we take, the people who want to get in will counter. We need to always police, always enforce, and yet always look to remedy the inadequacies of the policies which are in currently in place with an eye toward tomorrow in a just and systemized way.

Education

I would start with this- the Federal Government has about 500 mandates it has issued to State/local governments to pull off- and No Money to back it up. Seriously? IF that doesn't show you how dysfunctional a system we have is, how about a teacher in jail still being paid because it is illegal to fire her? Ever met a budget that actually went down? Ever seen a local school budget vote that didn't get taglined as "Do it for the Kids"? Tough to buy into that when 70% of a school budget goes to paying people who work about half a year, are tenured after 3 years, are removed by seniority- not talent, and will strike (not be there for the kids) if you so much as whisper you would reduce their benefits or ask them to contribute like all other private individuals towards their own health care.

I could go on- but the chase is this. ANY way to improve our model should be embraced and considered. ANY way to lessen the cost should be considered. ALL parties need to come together and address it on a broad level- not a year- to-year stopgap approach. The kids are the most important piece, and setting them up for success sets us ALL up for success. But they cannot be the reason we do not change, they need to be the reason we MUST change.

Idea-   ALL costs should be put back into the hands of the States to decide. ALL mandates should be from the state level. ALL costs should be paid for from tax revenue collected. When did we decide that we should pay property taxes to fund schools, pay for a laundry list of back to school items (some of which are for the class to benefit, not the individual child's need), pay for special trips above and beyond that, and then have to do fundraisers beyond that? LIVE WITHIN YOUR MEANS.

Idea-   When you vote for approving (or not) a school budget, there should be a couple things that happen. Why is school money spent putting signs up campaigning for the budget to be approved? Think it through; we pay tax money to buy signs to campaign to get more money from us. Really? What about let it pass on the merits. I don't mind a letter home to explain, but it should stop about there. Also if a budget fails, the result should be to freeze it at current levels. THAT would force school districts to make tough decisions and be creative. If the economy goes down and school budgets fail, the current system is to give a small increase as opposed to a big increase. How is that fair or just? So the school teachers and administrators get pay increases no matter what kind of economy there is?

Idea- What about using technology to save us money? Using an E-reader for text books would save tremendously. Use a states buying power to lower the per unit cost of one, put one in the hands of each child at a certain age(say 4th grade), put all their respective "books" on there for far less than buying texts outright cost, update yearly for even less, child is responsible for the return of the unit, and think about all the storage space and trees you would save in the process.

Website-   Department of Education (ED)

                http://www.ed.gov

Federal Trade Commission (FTC)

The FTC works for the consumer to prevent fraudulent, deceptive, and unfair business practices in the marketplace and to provide information to help consumers spot, stop, and avoid them.

So answer me this - in this land of freedom and opportunity-who would stand in the way of a corporate deal? Usually not the FTC, no matter what the size, scope or topic. The sad part is the FTC is meant, in part, to defend us (the US citizen) from corporate deal making that reduces our choices and threatens our markets/freedoms. Threatens? IF you only have 1 airline, they can charge any amount- the market becomes irrelevant since that one company IS the market. That is a threat. What about all the players in an industry acting similarly? What about where the reduction in companies- although still leaving room for multiple market choices yet would not allow for new competitors given natural impediments (oil for instance)? That is what I mean by threaten. And in this day and age- we have a new threat and you all know what it is- "too big to fail".

Too Big to Fail is the poster child statement for all the banks, investment houses, car companies, etc that just couldn't be allowed to fail for systemic risk. Really? What about the threat now then? Most of the very companies that are now around are bigger-so now what?

Idea- My answer is really simple- ***break them up***. When AT&T was this huge monopoly back in the early 80's it was split into about 7 separate entities and lived happily ever after. It could still compete- just differently. Why not do that with banking? Take the top 15 banks and break them up- the mid level tier of banks get a boost since the field would be leveled, the top banks would be forced to become lean and compete, the marketplace would benefit by true competition, and the consumer would benefit by better choices by banks much more responsive to what their needs are.

SO then WHY isn't the FTC saying anything like this? Is this not their very purpose? Why are they approving deals to make less competition and more too big to fail?

Federal Communications Commission (FCC)

Talk about social breakdown- think of the FCC. Remember the day when you could not curse during prime time? Politically correct takes on a whole different meaning when it comes to this archaic institution. Then to make matters worse, they sign off on huge communications deals which allow for the little business (radio station, service provider, etc) to suffer or go under while the big get ridiculously bigger. I am all for consolidation and economy-of-scale to a point, but at what point should we just say No and allow the markets to self police by allowing midsize to catch bigger competitors, small to become midsize, foreign to be held to same restrictions, etc? This isn't a huge deal- but is a piece of the breakdown of our social fabric, of our job pool, of our competitive nature. Why don't we let business compete on their merits, not on their sheer mass?

Side note- Remember when they sold us on cable TV? The idea was to have a pay-per-view TV and have it be Commercial Free. Have you looked at cable programming lately? So basically we pay now for the right to get programming and then get interruptions of commercials that make these stations additional money. WOW- did we get the short end of the stick.

Federal Communications Commission
445 12th Street SW, Washington, DC 20554
Phone: 1-888-225-5322
TTY: 1-888-835-5322
Fax: 1-866-418-0232
E-mail: fccinfo@fcc.gov

Transportation Safety Board (TSB) of the Dept of Transportation

The Transportation Safety Board- talk about outdated. All you need to know is that the "black boxes" they always refer to- are ORANGE. Like most things in Gov't, it is in need of a tremendous overhaul both in function and in mandate. Think of it this way- Once a crash happens, THAT is when they show up… Doesn't anyone else find that timing completely unacceptable? What about DO your job ahead of the curb, teach and police your turf to keep us safe, develop with private business the Best Practices for each respected industry so the result is a streamline of regulation (not just burdensome red tape), a higher safety outcome (your primary directive), and a much easier flow of business within the current economic, political, and threat-level of the day.

Idea- Mandate that the age of a fleet of planes stay under a certain range. Period. Mandate reinvestment in structures like rails and roads. Period. Go talk to ALL the businesses within your jurisdiction and find out their ideas and solutions- these BEST PRACTICES should be implemented system wide- both to streamline and protect the public that they serve. It isn't a burden, it is great business. Let them be part of the solution. Why? Because their costs would go down because of it. It is the nature of this wonderful idea called Capitalism.

U.S. Department of Transportation
1200 New Jersey Ave, SE
Washington, DC 20590
202-366-4000

Religion

WOW- where you been? Seems like when I was growing up-everyone went to church, it was what Sundays were for (in the morning). Most of my family friends were met there, common bond obviously. Now it seems churches are a distant past- mired in scandal, lack of impact in community, lack of voice in community, lack of current common and active solutions for everyday life.

A lot of the social problems we face today are a direct reflection of the lack of religion in our daily lives. The bigger question is "Can Religion get its MoJo back?". Time will tell. Today's unfortunate economic climate might be an opening of the door for religion to step through. Will it step up?

It doesn't help, in this second generation of duel incomes per household, that parents are around less and our children are being raised by daycare providers, nannies, and families try to make up for lost time on Sunday(if they aren't working already).

Idea- What about bringing back Blue Laws? Remember back in the day when Sundays were truly a day of rest? Wouldn't that help bring some time back into the family plan? Some rest for the productive? Business would still make their money on different days, save on the outlay on that day, and churches just might benefit by it in the process.

Another of the issues concerning Religion is the multiple angles people are pulled in. Allow a Muslim mosque, or not, in our American community based on current threat from that sect? Can Catholicism clean up its act from within? Can Religion get current and connect with today's social media nano-second generational demands?

The fiber of American is engrained with different cultures and religions, with various believes and focal points. Our country is stronger due to its diversity and we should never shy away from that. But the question is less of why would we ban a religion, it is more a question of why would we listen to what they have to say. Being Relevant in this day and age, this is the crucial piece. Gaining our trust as a collective society again will be difficult, but it is the critical element to putting balance back in our lives.

The first part is for religious leaders and sects to be worthy of their followers. The second part is for us to create a society in which participating in some form of local religion (or coordinated non-religion) is championed, not minimized. Separation of church and state was not intended to take us away from religion overall, just to minimize the churches direct control over us through political channels.

Supreme Court

The Supreme Court is the ultimate judge in our social fabric. What this group of 9 decides on every core issue is beyond appeal, sets precedent for future decisions, and is (should be) above politics.

We are about to put this to the ultimate test. They will review the "Obama care" Health Care Law in the Spring of 2012. IF they are above politics, they will give true credence to if it is legal and clarity to if it will in fact go forward and be implemented as is.

Given the fact that it will cause a huge swing in 16% of our total economy and set us on a possible new course within America, it is a critical juncture and possibly a social turning point.

Side note-   Supreme Court Justice Kagan was part of President Obama's staff when this Law was passed and was openly supportive and happy about its passage. She has not recused (removed) herself from this nationally critical deliberation within the Court. She is not mandated to do so, given the belief that Justices are elected for life and therefore will do what is "right" within the law, without concern for personal beliefs.

Like I said, this will be the ultimate test for the integrity and sovereignty of the Supreme Court and our belief in its ultimate justice within the Law. I hope their sense of what it right will lead them toward a fair outcome, as opposed to their personal sense of what they believe.

Congress- Senate and House of Representatives

WOW- gridlock in Washington more than I have ever seen in my lifetime, at a time when we need the government to be as highly functional as they can be.

Congress is made up of 100 Senate seats and 435 House seats. These elected politicians are sent to Washington for the greater good of their constituents and greater good of the Country. They need to work together to solve problems of their time. They have and are failing us at this.

Why won't you work together? Why won't you compromise? Why won't you deal in reality with solving issues daily, as opposed to letting them pile up over time? I hate to use the phrase of "kicking the can down the road" since it is tossed around as a buzz phrase to often as a sound bite- but why aren't we confronting the issues and dealing with them in real time? Why aren't the very people we send there doing what needs to be done?

Think of it this way- A General in the military is charged with taking a beachhead, mountain, front, or city. The General decides on the best strategy taking every aspect into consideration. The strategy is not without sacrifice or cost. The strategy is decided upon because it is the single best course of action- at a time when action is called for, when the goal is more valuable than the sacrifices made in acquiring that goal. At no time does the General not decide, not act, and not make getting that goal happen if the future of our country were hinging on it. SO why is Congress any different?

These elected officials are sent to Washington to get things done for us. Some moments in time have less urgent issues, simpler decisions, and easier money due to economic timing and tax receipts. Sometimes not- and now is one of those times. Their only goal is to fix our nation and put us on a path to a better life. Period. They cannot be concerned with re-election- that is ignoring the scale of the moment. They cannot be concerned about media spin- this is cow-towing to the broader pressures of our culture. They cannot put things off to another day, another time- that is shirking the very responsibility they have been assigned to resolve.

Remember the premise- IF you are not part of the solution, you are part of the problem. In this case ask yourself, is Congress acting as part of the solution or part of the problem?

Presidency vs. the President

Important point right out of the gate- The Presidency is the office and the President is a person. I say this to make a critical distinction in our social discourse.

The Presidency needs to be given respect, the Presidency is the leader of the free world, the Presidency needs to be BEYOND politics and out to solve the greater good more than anyone on the planet - due entirely to the country and resources they represent.

The President needs to earn respect and preserve the respect assigned to the Presidency. The President is the leader of the Free World and needs to speak, act, define that culture in a way they both represents our current core beliefs and our historical path as a Nation. The President needs to leave the politics behind once elected and do the job of representing ALL Americans. The President needs to be open to dialogue from both sides of the aisle, while acting on the best interests of us all.

True national leadership comes from a President who embraces the Presidency and supplies the connection between our two-party system. Our country is at a defining moment where we NEED that critical leadership, when it needs our President to put politics aside and define the moment within our culture by reaching out to both sides of the aisle and catalyzing what needs to be done to solve our ills.

The lack of true national leadership is my most frustrating issue. One cannot be elected, then turn and not represent us in critical moments like now. One cannot be put into office, then act like they hold a lower office with political bias. One cannot be put into the Presidency, then worry more about protecting your image, re-electability, your personal future. IF you do, you are by definition failing the very people who put you there, and sacrificing the future of the country you were trusted to lead.

Again, it goes back to the premise of the only one who will fix our nation is someone who truly doesn't want the job, but is put there just to get it done and go back to their life after the job is done.

Did you like what you read? Will you be a part of the solution?

Go To:

FixTheNation.com

Vote about the merit, or lack of, on ideas
Create new ideas
Give feedback for consideration
Post thoughts, concerns, or comments
Suggest or Glimpse topics to be covered in Volume Two
Link a sponsorship to a related sight
Sign the Guest book to hear about future releases

Remember the Purpose-

A Solution-based Social Media Outlet

<u>*Can we fix it?*</u>

That Answer is up to you- it is your voice, your vote, your country

"IF you aren't part of the Solution, then you are part of the Problem."

Thanks for reading, thanks for your involvement. Please take a minute and inform people you know about FixTheNation.com so they can have a louder voice as well.

www.ingramcontent.com/pod-product-compliance
Lightning Source LLC
Chambersburg PA
CBHW070234290526
45789CB00004B/1627